A NOTE TO PARENTS

When your children are ready to "step into reading," giving them the right books—and lots of them—is as crucial as giving them the right food to eat. **Step into Reading Books** present exciting stories or information reinforced with lively, colorful illustrations that make learning to read fun, satisfying, and worthwhile. They are priced so that acquiring an entire library of them is affordable. And they are beginning readers with an important difference—they're written on three levels.

Step 1 Books, with their very large type and extremely simple vocabulary, have been created for the very youngest readers. **Step 2 Books** are both longer and slightly more difficult. **Step 3 Books,** written to mid-second-grade reading levels, are for the child who has acquired even greater reading skills.

Children develop at different ages. **Step into Reading Books,** with their three levels of reading, are designed to help children become good—and interested—readers *faster.* The grade levels assigned to the three steps—preschool through grade 1 for Step 1, grades 1 through 3 for Step 2, and grades 2 and 3 for Step 3—are intended only as guides. Some children move through all three steps very rapidly; others climb the steps over a period of several years. These books will help your child "step into reading" in style!

Step into Reading

Tiger is a Scaredy Cat

by Joan Phillips
illustrated by Norman Gorbaty

A Step 1 Book

Random House New York

Library of Congress Cataloging in Publication Data: Phillips, Joan. Tiger is a scaredy cat. (Step into reading. A Step 1 book) SUMMARY: Tiger, a scaredy cat who is even afraid of the mice in his house, conquers his fear to help Baby Mouse. [1. Courage—Fiction. 2. Cats—Fiction. 3. Mice—Fiction] I. Gorbaty, Norman, ill. II. Title. III. Series: Step into reading. Step 1 book. PZ7.P5376Ti 1986 [E] 85-19673 ISBN: 0-394-88056-0 (trade); 0-394-98056-5 (lib. bdg.)

Manufactured in the United States of America 1 2 3 4 5 6 7 8 9 0

STEP INTO READING is a trademark of Random House, Inc.

Tiger is big.

Tiger is strong.

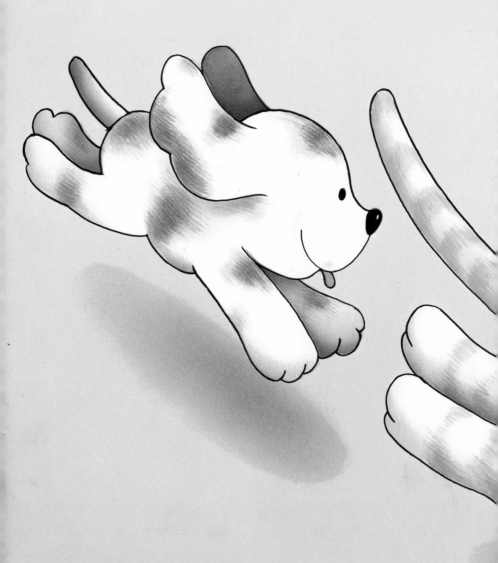

But Tiger is not brave.

He is scared of dogs.

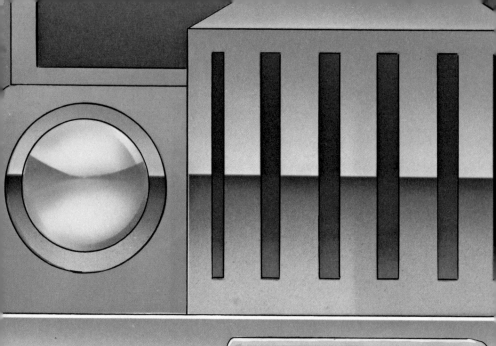
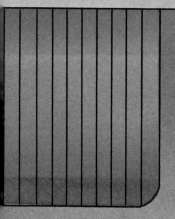

He is scared
of trucks.

He is scared
of the vacuum cleaner.

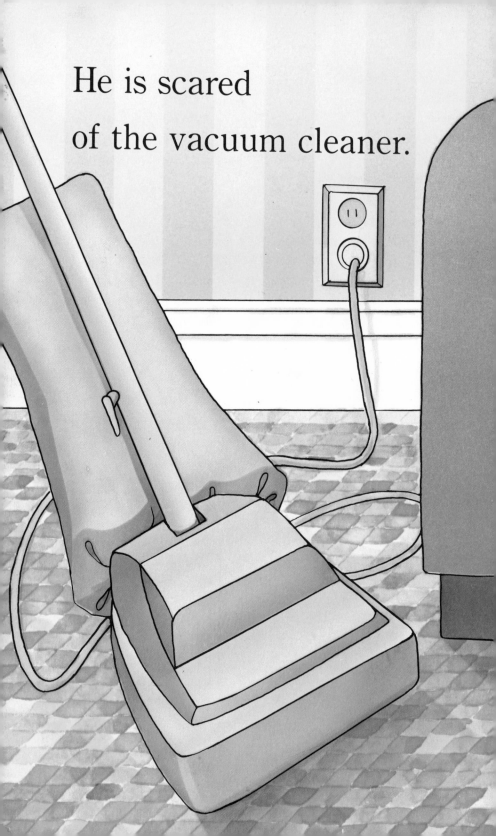

He is scared
of the dark.

Tiger is even scared
of the mice in his house.
What a scaredy cat!

There is nothing scary here.
There are no dogs,
no trucks,
no vacuum cleaners,
no mice.
And it is very sunny.
Tiger takes a cat nap.

The mice take a walk.

They do not see the cat.

Now they see the cat.
The mice are scared.
They run away.

Tiger sees the mice.

He is scared.

He runs too.

Baby Mouse falls.
"Waa! Waa!" he cries.

Tiger hears Baby Mouse.

21

"Waa! Waa!
I want to go home!"
cries Baby Mouse.
"Help me."

"No! I am too scared,"
says Tiger.

"Waa! Waa!
I want my mommy!"
cries Baby Mouse.
Tiger feels sorry
for Baby Mouse.

"Do not cry.
I will help you."

Tiger has to go
by a truck.

He has to go

by a dog.

He has to go
by the vacuum cleaner.

He has to go
down the dark stairs.

Tiger is scared.

But he helps anyway.

"Here is your mommy,"

he says.

"My baby!"
says Mother Mouse.
"Thank you! Thank you!"
says Father Mouse.

What a brave cat Tiger is!